The Gift of Poetry

A Walk Down A Path To Touch
The Mind, Soul And Heart

KWAJELYN LEWIS

Introduction

I wrote this book to express and share my love for poetry. It is my deep desire that when reading my poems that you will develop a true love for poetry. To me poetry is one of the most beautiful ways to express the many emotions that we have as humans. To write poetry is to express deep connections to the soul, heart and mind.

Table of Contents

The Heart

The Soul

The Mind

Queen

A beautiful melinated queen a lovely sight to be seen
So bold let the truth be told
Oh she is so bold with her quiet beauty it is her duty
To birth mankind you will see her you will find no other such
beauty she draws your attention your gaze
Looks so delicate but don't be deceived
A warrior's heart runs through her parts
Down her soul beautiful and bold

The Original

The first to be here proud, no reason to fear
or shed a tear no one to cut us down no
one to have to run from no one to have to escape
You came and what did you find a people of
great wisdom and great minds civilized a
spiritual system you didn't understand a
man in tune with nature and the land
benevolent beings hearts so kind

welcomed you in taught you many things
but you came to us with misgivings and
tricked us and got us to trust wicked thoughts
abound in your head you devised a plan put it in
motion took us by surprise you knew from the
beginning when you arrived in the land, and
people you would steal stop at nothing
rob, pillage, and kill you tried to justify it
all by giving us a book but when we took

a look it blinded us left us shook and on our
knees begging for forgiveness to someone
that never existed left us distraught even
though we fought our freedom at hand
a brave man stood to fight for his land
the original will always be nothing you can
do you see destined to be on top you can't do
anything we can't be stopped

My Tribe

My tribe will come with the right vibe a
spiritual kind a rare find able to seek
the unseen always aware and keen
able to glean the smallest nuance and
quick witted with the right response
deep thinkers' knowledge seekers truth

tellers cast speller's ancestor dwellers
no soul seller beautiful regalia
a sight to behold my tribe will hit the
the right stride take you along if you
have the right vibe

Can't Ignore Us

Can't ignore us won't restore us like our style
and our culture you are such a culture vulture
steal from others culture to try to build your
own to make yourself stand out and be known
can't ignore going to even the score we will be
restored destined to be on top never to be
stopped taken again we are going to win
You will be dropped you will be ignored

and stopped on the bottom you will be
kicked from the top exposed from head to
toes things will unravel spiral out of control as
you scramble to stay on top the trap you set
will be your downfall we will become big you
small but for what you did to us we are kind
hearted downright benevolent so you will be
all right in spite of your tumble, stumble your
fall

It's All a Distraction

It's all a distraction a created illusion hard
to find a solution or a resolution caught in a web
of lies and deception a hologram a multi trillion
dollar scam all like sheep meek little lambs
following along singing the same tune the same
song doing the wrong things seeking but not finding
going down a road that's winding afraid to face the
truth won't wake up from the matrix no way you

want to unplug from the reality of it all you are
headed for a great fall going to hit a wall
not able to stand tall all in all it's a wrap
not able to hold it together it's over people
are waking up the conscious are being born
the veil is lifted torn no more scorn no more
on the bottom headed to the top it's inevitable
incredible

You Can't Be Me

You can't be me a vision of loveliness
God created the best built like a palace oh so
fabulous trust me it just can't be this beautiful brown
sun-kissed by God you can't have my lips so kissable
big and round you walk around all over town trying to dress
like me but it will never be you see. Don't you know you can't
be me it is impossible I am unstoppable so go ahead
and try you know you not fly not royalty not heaven sent
but hell bent on trying to be me you can't be me
I'm righteous

full of light bold strong full of might a warrior ready and
armed for the fight like a thief in the night trust and believe
we gon be alright gon rise to the top these sun-kissed
people the real ones the woke ones the real fighters
the ones reaching towards the universe
the ones you said were cursed gon burst on the scene
gon take control gon set things right
gon show you whose boss
gon take our rightful place gon win the race

Scammers and Schemers

Scammers and Schemers big time dreamers
trying to get paid hoping to get laid
Gon end up getting sprayed not intending
to be laid out prostrate for all to view thought
you could get yo hustle on talk was bold and
strong went on for so long it was totally wrong
now you are singing a jail house song
You met the game changer the bomb dropper

the heart stopper the throat popper
the head knocker the world rocker the snake
charmer now you somber what a bomber
hope the lesson was learned not to burn
the ones you say you loved not to play such
a game so you feel no shame don't be the blame
don't be so lame learn a lesson from this game
changer

You Must not Know About Me

You must not know about me I am
the woman of your dreams It would seem
that if I were not in your dreams and real
I would make you light up shine and beam
come out of my dreams meet me for real
seal the deal let me show how love really
feels let me steal your heart right from
the start take a chance get to know me

see us go through life's dance with it's
twist and turns, twirls and swirls ups and
downs ins and outs over and on tops
handling the flops, the sudden drops
the missteps, the stumbles even the
rumbles and tumbles You must not
know about me for I exist in your
dreams

Jamaican Girl

Jamaican girl with your beautiful brown skin
Jamaican girl with your jet-black curls
little Jamaican girl running on the beach
stopping to twirl in the sun play and have
fun little Jamaican girl sweet little voice

pretty eyes so innocent and bright
picking mangos that are just right
back to the beach to watch the sea gulls
take flight little Jamaican girl you are
out of sight

Tricky

Tricky with your talk so smooth who
are you what kind of dude with your
good looks you exude so elusive so
slick you and yo tricks out to get what
you can get out to win all the bets
live the good life with take another's
wife be a snake in the grass out

just to get some ass you are quick
on the run going out just for fun
seeking your next mark but don't get
got caught with a thot burnt
to a crisp
tricky

The Heart

Didn't You Know You Carried Me

Didn't you know you carried me through
When I was lost didn't know what to do
When tears streamed down my
face you whipped them away with
delicacy and grace When I was so
sad spirit so broken you picked me up

gave me love and a token beautiful
words were spoken in my ear to
give me hope and take away the
fear guide me strengthen me
steer my boat got me back on my
feet spirit lifted outlook shifted

You Carried Me

You have been apart of me for so long
Standing there big and strong helping
me to weather the storm life has
hit us hard but you fought on carried
me along the battle roared on yet you

stood strong bound and determined to
not just to win the battle but the war we've made
it thus far climbed hills, crossed deep waters
you never left me behind you carried me through
the depths of time you will always be mine

You are always on my Mind

Always on my mind constantly in my thoughts
jumping in my spirit I continuously feel it
You never know it goes unsaid the thoughts
of you kept my mind fed memories of how
things used to be the joy of your presence
you see these thoughts and memories
never flee from me always on my mind
stirring up things I want to forget

regret things that could
change lessons learned so much
concern a desire does burn
wish I had a turn to say what was never said a
chance to make it right a chance to fight
another day a chance to see things
your way for you are always on my
mind

Just Be Thankful

Just be thankful no matter what comes
your way count your blessings everyday
say to yourself I'm still here there is no reason
to fear if I must cry and the tears fall there
is always someone you can call to pick you up
to spread some cheer to comfort and take and
take away fear to give a word of encouragement
to give a smile and sentiment just be
thankful

Take My Hand

Take my hand hold it tight protect me
with all your might take my hand take
with you to the highest height
in search of a spiritual light a light
so bright our souls at its sight quicken we
know it's right take my hand hold on for dear life
dispel the strife because of this soul stirring
light the light that made things right take my
hand and don't ever let go for I love you

so

Will You Still Love Me When I Grow Old

Will you still love me when we grow old
will you still bring me beans in my favorite
green bowl look at you with a look that touches
your soul will you still hold my hand to cross the
street will you still dance with me without missing a
beat will you be around to continue the heat to climb
the hills together there will be no defeat by this time
in our lives we will finally receive life's gifts and treats

Yes, I will Love You
When You are Old

Yes, I will love you when you are old bring you your

blanket and shield you from the cold I'll hold your

hand and smile bold and cook up a batch of beans

to bring you in your favorite green bowl and give you the

truth to fill your soul I'll hold you in my arms like I used to

do when we were young and hold you tight

I'll hum to you a song, kiss you good night and talk

to you so sweet never harsh impatient or to scold

For we have grown old together and time is oh

so short just a little to longer the kingdom in sight

this battle we want have to fight I will sing your favorite

song to you all day long though it may be out of tune
my dear I hope you won't mind for it will be hard for you to
hear but I love you so my precious precious dear
now your hair has turned gray, but you don't have to
dismay for it will attest to the wisdom you have
found and now that your eyes have grown dim and the
sparkle is gone away I will read you your poems before
the lights go out and things are done we
will sit and remember times gone by and I will wrinkled skin
and eyes

I Regret

I regret the day we met for the journey has
been long and hard got off from the
beginning on the wrong start
continuing to break each other's heart
say mean things treat each other bad always
seem mad trying to pretend one day we are
going to win what then will it finally change
will things be rearranged with no regret no
need to fret or will things remain the same with
regret

Complicated

Complicated so complicated we make things
so complicated in life things are under rated
our lives intertwined the blind leading the blind
searching but can't find life so short
running out of time we grow old things continue
to implode can't seem to fix it things are in a
mess all twisted up at best bliss seems so far
away lost for words don't know what to say

just want to get away lay it all down let it
rest can't change the past or turn back time
on the drop of a dime should be in a good
place aging like fine wine instead so
complicated so complicated under rated
just complicated broken, words unspoken
it was broken from the start

You Don't Know Who I am

You don't know me who I really am
you don't know me you think I'm
a sham disingenuous self-absorbed
doing things my way doing what I want
you don't know me from my heart you
didn't know me not even from the start
you want to be apart of me want to know
who I am want to see what I was all about

but you never delved deeply into my mind
never took the time never asked questions
didn't want to go that far it is just so bizarre
you don't know me who I really am
knowledge beyond college research
already done you don't know
me I don't even really exist

When You Come

When you come it's sunshine and soft gentle
breezes birds sing in trees I see the color
of the fall leaves to look upon you I am
pleased you bring me joy like a child with
a new toy you've never known what your
presences means don't notice how you

change the scene the joy on faces the light
you bring the way you make people beam
no illusions no unfilled dreams you lift
everyone's spirit you brighten up gloomy
days when you come

Missed

You are so missed your gentle touch soft kiss
that would bring bliss your smile your style
your gon be alright child your voice that demanded
attention hanging on every word you mentioned
oh the joy you brought to my life you are missed
even some strife your presence made the world
a better place to made me feel happy, secure
and safe you are so missed your smile
your kiss your style

When It's Time to Say Goodbye

When it's time to say goodbye
to walk away to let go when everything
is no more I will leave and let go no
looking back no angry attacks
no regrets no flack just a gentle glance and
a slow turn trying to hide the hurtful burn
tears may fall hearts may be broken but our

love is gone only memories are left of what
was us no need to discuss there is not us
no more time is left our time has been passed our
relationship placed on a far away shelf
I left you; you left me we didn't last no
growing old together no making things better
when it's time to let go just exhale and let

go

Anger

Tried to soothe your soul say the right thing even
gave you some bling tossed money your way
tried to save the day but not enough to restore the
trust hurt feelings evil dealings disrespect what the
heck tried to put me in check shut me down no
life about to drown no life to be saved just anger, rage

trapped bird in a cage broken wings can't sing what's
going to happen to this if it truly comes to a head
will we make it or will this relationship fall dead
Things already shifted found a voice made a choice
sought out Source screamed to the Universe heart
about to burst it can't get worse you to be first

You Stir Something Deep within my Soul

You stir something deep within my soul
you reach the depths of my being
you see who I am who I could be
you allow me to be me I am accepted
I am believed pure and fresh I am willing to
give you my best no test to be given no
doubt cast the deep soul stirring will last

for you came from my past cast among
the stars in the depths of the deep dark universe
you emerged like a flame burning bright
a beautiful and special light
eyes opened from a blindless sight
things changed it's so right
you stir something deep within my soul

Over the Years

Over the years struggle, tears, fears, sneers, and abuse
Misuse hurt feelings broken hearted right from the start
no real kiss what a shame a real diss an awful miss ruined
no bliss but here we stand hand in hand a real ban our
clan so many years gone by still we wake up and try, try
to find true happiness set a purpose reach a goal neither

one wanting to fold throw in the towel hang it up turn and
run kiss it all goodbye give up don't even give a fuck this
really sucks don't even try ask myself why tell myself no
lies look to the heavens try to think of something cleaver
our relationship I will never sever with you I will stay forever

When You Look at Me

When you look at me what do you really see
why do you feel that you need to kill me
why can't you just let me be
tried to get away, be on my own
but you just couldn't leave
me alone
Built Tulsa, Rosewood, Sweet Auburn
Pennsylvania Avenue and other towns
But through your anger and jealousy you burned,
Bombed, destroyed and tore them down

thought it was because I am black, beautifully brown
but that's not true, that's not why you do
what you do the color of my skin has nothing to
do with it at all it's not the reason for my fall
when you see me, I remind you of times past when
I was first and you were last you came to a land
With people so black so dark a people with
benevolent hearts, met the people with the
spirit of God

you set at the feet of the true masters just to
learn and steal our knowledge and people
you sorry bastards brought us to this land,
done all you can had your knee on my neck
and my back, both figuratively and physically
tied my hands put a strangle hold on me
just to break me economically
you got me hanging from a tree just because
you think you can it's time to stop, take a stand,

take back this land built by my ancestors with
blood, sweat and tears it belongs to us and we
are going to fight without fears this type of mankind,
this type of crew continues to slaughter there is
no changing you, there is no compromise all I
get are continuous lies you seek my vote but
in the streets the cops continue to kill and choke
reparations I demand, but all I get is an empty hand
while others across this land, get everything they demand

my ancestors blacker than a thousand midnights expect
me to stand up and fight not to beg for equal rights
for I know there is no other man that is equal to
the Gods and Goddess of the dark land
So, that's what you see when you look at me
the reason you stole, destroyed, and continue to
kill so, here is the real deal, something to know
God or Goddess like me
that's for sho!!

Choose Me

Choose me with my hips so round with my
Skin so golden beautiful and brown
choose me with my haughty attitude
And beauty that exudes a charm and wit
a body so fit personality that won't quit
like to get it cronk like to get it lit talk a
little you know put on a show let things

flow choose me will do you no harm
no need for alarm I'll have yo back keep
you on track be your help meet be your
lover in the sheets you be my warrior in
the streets bringing the heat choose me
and you will never look back
choose me

Heartache

Heartache heartbreak for God's sake
Don't you cause me no heartache or
heartbreak don't you trample
on my fragile heart don't you just come
in here to sample my love runs so
deep don't you even think you gon

creep better sleep with one eye open
if you think my love you gon sink
you better think twice I ain't gon be nice
so don't you bring me no heartache
for God's sake

Missed

You are so missed your gentle touch soft kiss
that would bring bliss your smile your style
your gon be alright child your voice that demanded
attention hanging on every word you mentioned
oh the joy you brought to my life you are missed

even some strife your presence made the world
a better place made me feel happy, secure
and safe you are so missed your smile
your kiss your style

Missed But Not Gone

Oh how I miss your smile oh how I
miss your style oh how I miss
your embrace oh how I miss your
grace oh how I miss your beautiful face
oh how I miss hearing you call my name
oh how I miss the advice you gave oh
how I miss your gentle touch oh how

I miss your such and such oh how I
miss your bright smile it would light up the
room and remove all the gloom oh my sweet
dear you left me too soon left me with sweet
memories that bloom from within you can't
possibly know how much you are missed
oh that you could come back for just one last

kiss an embrace a soft gentle touch it would
fill my heart rejuvenate my life take away
the strife fill me full of life come back my sweet
loved one to make a lasting memory for me
to hold fast but you have passed and life must
go on I will hold tight and continue to fight the good
fight until we meet again among the stars

Oh My God

Oh what you do to me got me in a whirl wind
going around and around I spin head in a
daze walking around in thought filled haze
spending my days thinking about you
Oh My God the things you say to me
take my breath away you see got

me over here lost in deep thoughts
of the possibilities of what could be
you and me is this a dream a possible reality
It's you I have always sought feelings that won't
be fought don't even know if this is real

or if you are you taking a blind leap of
faith sight unseen no in between
leading with my heart I knew from the
start I am giving you my heart
Oh My God

What Would I Do Without You

I ask myself what I would do without you
it's a complicated thought deep in my
soul I have sought to find in the crevices of my
mind spent so much time in search of the
answer of all times not a clue of what I'd do
without you no feeling of grandeur no outlook

of soaring high only deep sighs and goodbyes
tears, fears, anger, and sneers forgiveness doesn't
exist only bald up fist and nasty tricks you oh
so slick oh so sick what would I do without you
live my life without strife what would I do without

you

You Are

You are the air I breath the cool breeze
that blows through the trees
the apple of my eye if you were to
leave this earth I'd surely die
you are the wings of a dove flying
so high above for you my dear are
pure love

you are the sparkle in my eye but
should you depart from the earth
I'd surely die
you are the laughter of happy children
at play you are the sun the break of day
you are the whispers in lovers ear
you are their tears
you are the calm voice within that
quiets my soul

you are the arms that tightly hold the
hand of a loved one that has grown
old
you are the one that I live for the air I breath
oh my dear don't depart for should you go
or when you die I shall become a dove and we
shall find rest above.

The Soul

Game Changer

Game changer snake charmer
Bomb dropper can't stopper
In like a lamb out like a lion mover and shaker
No enemy taker bone breaker like boss a boss
in charge not false
Like a wrecking ball standing tall lifting queens up
straightening crowns fixing frowns when they are
down guns cocked daggers tucked away
on ready everyday game changers don't
play they play, pray, and slay dressed to kill

looking fresh always doing her best better than
the rest got your back help you stay on
track knowledgeable about many facts a leader
a truth speaker a knowledge seeker always digging
deeper on code with her people helping to guide
staying in stride not full of pride but head held high
able to make a way out of no way make the sunshine
on a cloudy day wipe away tears quiet fears,
sneers, and jeers game changers

Triple Threat

Triple threat you bet get ready
set on the go you know just
got it going in on so talented
and strong nothing you touch
goes wrong sharp as a tack

stay on track no slack
never wack the original not a
copy never sloppy you can't
stop me triple threat you
absolutely bet

Sunday Morning Blues

Sunday morning blues I got these Sunday morning blues
don't know what I'm gon do about these
Sunday morning blues
Sunday morning blues I got these Sunday morning blues
I see you form my windowpane I feel so drained
I see you dressed from head to toe I see you rushing
through the church doors
Sunday morning blues I got these Sunday morning blues
Preachers ready to preach such bad news ready to preach

What he don't know this false prophet got to go
Sunday morning blues I got these Sunday morning blues
Brothas and sistas heads held high hanging on every low
down lie
Sunday morning blues I got these Sunday morning blues
When I try to tell you the truth you buck turn tail and run
You even tell me to go to hell don't you know you gonna
fail

Sunday morning blues I got these Sunday morning blues
You don't have a clue about my Sunday morning blues
You gon get your due if you don't realize you being
lied to
Head held high don't want you to die why don't you give
the truth a try stop listening to those lies listen to the
real prophets prophesy
Sunday morning blues I got these Sunday morning blues

I know what I'm gon do about these Sunday morning blues
I'm gon give you the truth from the truth seekers
With the real news
Then I won't have no Sunday morning blues because
You gon get my drift and run really swift gon finally
Get it right from the truth seekers that are oh
So bright with the knowledge from the motherland

The Candies of Life

May your years be more sweet than tart
May the energy from the stars burst
in your heart
may your day be filled with more laughter
than tears
may you face your fear like the three musketeers
may you always remember that you are

a smarty and your ideas are good and hearty
may you be the friend when a boat
is sinking and there is little hope
be the one to throw out a life saver
and let that someone ride in your
boat

Color Me Brown

Color me brown like the color of caramel flavored
creamed coffee
color me brown like the taste of sweet toffee
color me brown like roasted pecans hot from
the oven
color me brown like the color of sand
in the motherland
color me brown like the soil of mother earth

color me brown like the tallest mahogany tree
color me brown like sweet Georgia tea
color me brown like hot buttered toast
color me brown like a Sunday roast
color me brown that's the color that's the most
I don't mean to boast but color me brown
like the universe planned
color me brown like my ancestor's hands that

toiled in the dark rich soil as they worked the
land
lessons we can look back on and learn
so, color me brown from the lightest of light
to the darkest of dark as I make a difference grow
up and follow my heart

To Teach

To teach means so many things
you must become to see your
students though you guide them
you protect them help them make
decisions on what to do and over
the years you look back on all the
lives you touched and hope that

a difference has been made you
hope that they listened to what
you had to say and when it's
all said and done and it's time
to bid everyone adieu you look
back with pride and joy for choosing to
reach a child for choosing to
teach

Namesake

When you were born your parents thought to
name you after me don't know why couldn't
see why you deserved to be named after me
but just the same the name came and you
wear it well for you child with the fighting
spirit gave the name life for many causes
have your way and you didn't flinch didn't
turn away stood your ground rolled with

the punches don't fit the usual mold didn't
fold so my namesake that gave the name new
life to our name you wear it well bring it
no shame namesake fight on lift the banner
high fight the powers that be until the fighting
ends and a new chapter begins and when that
day comes and the battle ends and there
is not more fight in you the good fight you fought
time to bid us adieu namesake you I love you

Ancestors

Ancestors that walked the motherland
A beautiful black clan awesome
band spread across the land
far and wide full of pride
built the pyramids and left it written
in the stones left the bones of the great
kings and queens left knowledge for us

to live by to keep us alive to help us strive to
help us thrive the original people from the beginning of
time come walk among us be our spiritual guide whisper
in our ear teach us what we need to know never
leave us never let us go we will honor you and
keep you in our heart

The Stars are Within You

The stars are within the ancestors
your kin the beginning there since the beginning
of time in the abyss the deep the sublime the
deep ringing down in your soul the bell sounding
the chime look within to find the source your
guide your way to your higher self the true
you the one you need to be look within for
the stars are within

Old Hands

Old hands have a story to tell old hands wisdom
never fails old hands have life lessons to impart
old hands have cared for me from the start
old hands calm my fears old hands dried my
tears old hands stood up for me against the
sneers old hands raised me to be kind old hands
helped me to find my way old hands had funny
things to say old hands always made my day

old hands taught me how to pray old hands taught me how to keep the faith and to not stray to read the Bible everyday old hands singing spiritual songs singing on the porch all day long continuing to teach right from wrong teaching before long I was missing old hands for old hands have gone home

It's Us

It's us with our melanin skin dripping from
The outside all the way within brown and jet
black skin it's always been us with our black
magic our swagger cool demeanor benevolent.
spirit can't kill it you know you feel it
would do anything to get it steal it
you get a hold of it and deal it

make money off of us you create such
distrust it's us thc original crew
you refuse to give us our due
can't even sue just cry the blues
but a change gon come it will be
done because it has always been

us

Be Who You Are

Be who you are for it is written in the stars
follow the right path take the time to smile
and laugh follow your dreams reach your goals
take a chance to be brave and bold
let no one stand in your way
no matter what they say open your eyes
be true to yourself face your fears

head on follow the journey no matter how long
stay the course don't veer to the left or right fight
for your dream be who you are be strong
you can't go wrong when you are being
who you are you will out shine any star love
and be who you are

Unity

Unity is a family
unity of us black
people joining together hand
in hand intertwined forever across this
land and our home the motherland
a strong ban sister and brother
mother and father caring for each other

making your problems mine
trying to settle a score placed upon our
ancestors coming up with a plan to help a
black man giving us all a leg up allowing
us bolder placing a fire inside time to rise
summon that fighting spirit don't let
it die reach down feel it use it lift us

up build, educate before it's too late
don't berate your sister or brother encourage
invest build for the future it's not time to rest
we after all are the salt of the earth no
need to search or take others lead
take heed be the one to bring unity, community, and pride

About the Author

Kwajelyn Lewis is from Baltimore, Maryland by way of Macon, Georgia. Kwajelyn is a graduate of Spelman College in Atlanta, Georgia. Kwajelyn has a Bachelor of Arts degree in Early Childhood Development. Kwajelyn serves as an educator and has been teaching for thirty years. Kwajelyn is currently a first grade educator in the state of Maryland.

9 798985 291711